Tunisia Travel Guide

By
Mike Gerrard

PUBLISHED BY
Blue Sky Books
Cambridgeshire, England, and Green Valley, Arizona, USA.

Table of Contents

GETTING TO KNOW TUNISIA

Tunisia is the smallest country in North Africa, yet is one of its most popular holiday destinations - and rightly so, as it has some of the best beaches along the southern shores of the Mediterranean. It is warm and sunny almost all the time (though nights can be cold), and has some very fertile regions in the north and the centre of the country, in contrast to many people's expectations.

It does have desert too, as the south of Tunisia includes the northern part of the Sahara Desert, giving visitors chance to see the rugged desert scenery, which can be both barren and beautiful. Riding a camel in the desert really does make you feel like Lawrence of Arabia for a short while.

THE PEOPLE

Another reason for Tunisia's popularity is the friendliness of its people. Most of them cannot do enough to help visitors, and like many Arab countries it is renowned for its hospitality.

The desert dwellers here are the Berbers, whose roots go back at least 3000 years and who pride themselves both on their hospitality and their sense of humour. These elements have come down to the modern population, which is almost 11 million, with almost all of them being Arabs or Berbers, or a mix of the two.

The culture is not exclusively Arabic, though, as you will soon see. There has been a great French and Italian influence here, evident in things like food and architecture, so European visitors usually feel much more at home here than in other African countries.

Tunisia has always been much more tolerant and liberal than other Muslim countries, a fact which has not always gone down well with its Arab neighbours. There is a more relaxed attitude towards alcohol, for instance, which Tunisians are forbidden to drink under Islamic law but which is freely available to visitors in hotels and most restaurants.

Nevertheless, visitors must remember that it is an Islamic country, and it is important to dress more respectfully away from the beach. It would cause offence and be seen as an insult if you tried to visit a mosque, for example, while wearing shorts or a skimpy top. Tolerance has to work both ways.

Tunisian Girl Serving Tea in Matmata

MOSQUES

One of the distinctive sounds of a Muslim country like Tunisia is the call to prayer from the mosque. The sound wails out from the minarets five times a day, the first at dawn. This call is the *adhan* and is made by the muezzin, an official of the mosque. He is actually saying things like 'Allah is most great', 'Come to prayer', 'come to salvation' and 'There is no god besides Allah'.

The more devout Muslims will stop what they are doing and pray at the appointed times, so be prepared to see this sometimes in shops or other public places. Some shop owners briefly close to enable them to say their prayers. Mosques are generally closed to non-Muslims, but some open their courtyards to the public though you may not be allowed to go any further than this.

CLIMATE
The northern part of Tunisia, where most of the holiday resorts are based, has a typical Mediterranean climate. The summers are dry and hot - sometimes quite a bit hotter than you may have been used to if you have visited Spain or Greece, for example. In winter the north remains mild, and a little rain does fall. The further south you go, towards the Sahara, the hotter and drier it becomes.

Camel in Douz, Tunisia

WILDLIFE
It won't be long before you see your first camel, and maybe even be tempted to ride on one. They have a reputation for being bad-tempered, but are fascinating animals, well-adapted to the harsh life of the desert. They can go many days without food or water, they have three eyelids and those long eyelashes to protect their eyes against the sand, while pads of skin under their feet enable them to walk on the sand without sinking into it.

Although there are wild camels in the world, you won't see any in Tunisia. Even those you may spot in the middle of nowhere will belong to someone, perhaps a Berber. The proper wild animals of Tunisia include deer, wild boar, jackals, foxes, hares and that well-known pet, the gerbil. Don't expect to see too many of these, however, even on a desert safari. You may be thankful not to see snakes and scorpions, as while they do have these in Tunisia they are mostly in the south of the country.

SETTLING IN
MONEY MATTERS
The Tunisian currency is the dinar, usually shown as TD. This is divided into 1000 millemes (mills), which is why you will sometimes see prices written as TD1.500. That's one dinar and five hundred mills, or 1.5 dinar. It's a soft currency which means it can't be imported or exported.

Be careful not to change more than you think you will need. When you leave you can only change back up to 30% of what you changed into dinars in the first place, with a maximum limit of TD100. You also need the bank receipts to show how much you did change, so do your sums carefully, or change money bit by bit as you go. You can't spend any left-over dinars once you're beyond passport control. You can always save them for your nest holiday, although it is then illegal to bring TDs back into the country!

There are plenty of places to change money, at banks and bureaux de changes, and you should have no problem exchanging sterling, other major currencies or Thomas Cook travellers' cheques.

Credit cards are widely used in hotels, restaurants and shops, and can be used to draw money at a bank. There are cash machines in most large towns, connected to the various international cash networks. If your card links to one of these, then the pin number you use at home will be valid here.

Tunisian Dinar

HEALTH AND HYGIENE

Tap water in Tunisia is safe to drink but some people don't like the taste and tend to stick to bottled water.

Take a little bit of care with what you eat, if you want to avoid stomach problems. If you buy any fruit then wash it if you can't peel it. Ice-cream is tempting but in some places it may have been allowed to melt and then re-frozen, which can make you ill. Shellfish sometimes cause problems, but generally the food is fine unless you choose to eat in very basic places.

If you do get a stomach bug, remember to drink lots of water to replace the fluids you lose. Most tummy bugs only last 24-48 hours, but if yours persists then ask your hotel to recommend a doctor. Tunisia has an excellent health service.

Most people have no worse trouble than trying to cope with the heat. Keep covered up, and slap on the sunscreen regularly. Drink more water than you would normally, to replace the sweat, and try not to drink too much alcohol during the day. If you get a slight headache it might be the start of dehydration, so again drink lots of water to get back to normal.

SHOPS AND SERVICES

Shops are generally open Monday to Friday from about 8-9am to midday, and then open again about 2-3pm until 6pm or so. On Saturday they open in the mornings only.

Souvenir shops tend to stay open as long as there are souvenir-hunters around, usually quite late in the summer. In summer banks usually only open from 7.30-11am because of the heat, and at other times will also open for a spell in the afternoons. In most tourist resorts there is usually one bank which opens on a Saturday morning, so if you need one then ask your holiday rep or at your hotel.

Shopping for Ceramics in Djerba

PHONING HOME

It's easy to phone home from Tunisia but calls are comparatively expensive, especially from a hotel. You can dial from most public phones but will need a stock of dinar coins, though some take phone cards that you buy from Post Offices. It's cheaper after 9pm and on Sundays. Dial 00 first followed by your country code.

CRIME AND EMERGENCIES

Tunisia is by and large a very safe country. Islamic laws are as strict on theft as they are on alcohol, so the vast majority of Tunisians are brought up to be very honest - you might not think so when they try to sell you a carpet, but that's bargaining, not theft! It is incredibly rare to come across anything as serious as a mugging.

Each hotel has contact with a local doctor, so seek their advice if you encounter medical problems. Otherwise dial 190 for an ambulance, 197 for fire and 198 for police.

GETTING AROUND

Taxis are a cheap and easy way of getting around within the resorts, but are expensive to get from one town to another. Buses and trains are usually good and quite cheap, and there is a Metro between Sousse and Monastir. Buy your tickets from the train or metro station, or on the bus.

CAR HIRE

Few things are expensive in Tunisia, but car hire is. It can be arranged through your hotel, but be prepared to pay through the nose. It would be dangerous to consider going towards the desert on your own, so if you want to see it stick to the organised tour.

LANGUAGE

English is used quite widely in most tourist towns, but more people speak French. A few basic words in Arabic:

Yes	iyeh
No	la
Please	men fadhlek
Thank you	shukran
Hello	asalam alaykum
(to which the response is wa alaykum asalam)	
Goodbye	ma'as salama

WHAT DOES IT ALL MEAN?

Caleche	A horse-drawn carriage
Hammam	Public bath-house
Kasbah	A fortress or citadel
Ksibah	A small fortress
Medressa	An Islamic school, like a seminary
Medina	The city, but specifically the old city
Minaret	The tower in a mosque
Muezzin	Mosque official who makes the call to prayer
Ribat	Fortified Islamic monastery
Souq	Market

Arabic and English on a Street Sign in Tunis

THE BEST OF TUNISIA
BEACHES
With nearly 900 miles of Mediterranean coastline, there are bound to be a few good beaches! The best are obviously where tourism has developed, in the resorts from Hammamet south to Monastir. The main beach at Monastir has an especially impressive setting, backed by the imposing town fortress.

The Beach at Sousse

THE DESERT
No-one should visit Tunisia without getting at least a glimpse of the desert, whether for one day or, if you can spare the time, for a longer safari. Not for nothing was the country chosen as the setting for the film The English Patient. You may never be as close to the Sahara again, so make the most of your chance to see it.

Douz, the Gateway to the Sahara

TUNISIA TRAVEL TIP
Haggling is a way of life in Tunisia, so if you thing you've got the hang of it in the local shops, try it out on the taxi drivers and see what happens!

HANDICRAFTS
There are some fine examples of craft items for sale in the country, especially jewellery and hand-made carpets. Good quality does not come cheap, of course, but it's usually a lot cheaper if you're prepared to haggle. See the Shopping section for some advice here. You will see a great deal of silver for sale because silver is the only pure metal, according to the Prophet Mohammed. One very common design is the Hand of Fatima, as Fatima was the Prophet's favourite daughter,

AND MANY MORE...
There are many suggestions for other things you 'must do' while you're in Tunisia, and here are just a few:
* Eat a traditional dish like couscous or brik - but do it the traditional way too, with your fingers.
* Take a ride on a camel.
* Have at least one haggling session in the local market.
* Even if you've come for a beach holiday, you ought to see at least one of the country's many splendid ancient ruins.

* Allow plenty of time to visit the ancient medinas, and explore the back streets where some of the more unusual souks can be found.
* Try the local liquor if you're offered it: thibarine. It's made in the village of Thibar near Dougga, and will take your breath away!
* Take an evening stroll around the quays in the resorts, and enjoy a promenade with the locals. Or just watch from a nearby café.

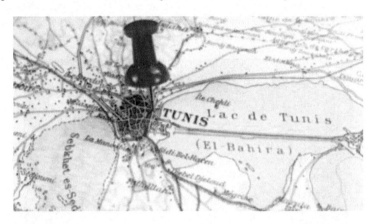

TUNIS

Nearby Carthage was the Roman capital of the region, but when the Arabs invaded in 698 they made Tunis their capital. They built the medina which was the city, with nothing outside its walls for another thousand years or so. Inside there were up to 100,000 people living, whereas today the population is down to 15,000 - and about 14,000 of them seem to own carpet shops! The other 1,000 all have a brother who owns one.

The medina was made a World Heritage Site in 1981, emphasising its importance, and no visit to Tunisia would be complete without a wander round its side streets. The other great attraction in the city is the Bardo Museum, which even non-museum lovers admit to being impressed by. It is the best museum in North-West Africa.

Apart from the Bardo Museum, which is about two miles west of the centre, most of the sights are inside the medina. The Ville Nouvelle is the 'New Town' built by the French when they took over in 1881, and here is the modern life of Tunis - the banks, the offices and the cafés. It's a busy but pleasant area to stroll around in, especially in the evening when people are promenading prior to a night on the town.

Other pleasing aspects of the city are Lake Tunis, where you can sometimes see flamingoes in winter, and the fact that Tunis has several parks. Belvedere Park to the north of the city centre sits around a hill, from the top of which there are splendid views.

TUNISIA TRAVEL TIP
Carpet touts are persistent and some are devious. It's probably safest to refuse all invitations to come into shops, look at views, stop for a coffee or anything else. Most usually end up in a carpet shop.

At the Bardo Museum in Tunis

THINGS TO SEE AND DO
*** The Medina. Make sure you've got a map as the old town is huge, containing many mosques and souks. Some of the souks specialise in such things as jewellery, gold, silver and spices.

*** Bardo Museum. The other big 'must see' in Tunis, and included on organised excursions, is this, the best museum in the country and the second-biggest in Africa after the museum in Cairo. It is housed in a one-time palace, and that alone is worth seeing, but inside is a fine collection of Carthaginian, Christian, Islamic and Roman remains - especially the wonderful collection of Roman mosaics.

** Great Mosque ez-Zitouna. On Rue Jamaa Zitouna in the medina, this is the largest and holiest mosque in Tunisia. It may even have been built when the city was founded in 698. The courtyard is open to non-Muslims daily except Friday and Sunday.

BEACHES
Go to La Marsa at the end of the TGM train line where the best city beaches are to be found.

Tunis, in the Medina

CARTHAGE

Carthage is a suburb of Tunis, but quite a select one. Not only are there expensive villas and embassies, but the President himself lives here in the Presidential Palace, right next to the ruins of Carthage.

It has to be said that the ruins of Carthage are not among the country's major sites. This can be a disappointment to some visitors, as almost everyone knows the name of Carthage - even if you don't always know why - yet the remains here are not nearly as impressive as the much lesser-known Tunisian sites such as Dougga and El Djem.

Having said that, you can't come to Tunis and not visit Carthage, to see the remains for yourself. There is more still to be discovered about Carthage, but it isn't likely to happen for a while as other remains are buried under those expensive modern villas and beneath the Presidential Palace.

There are two main reasons why people remember Carthage from history lessons at school. The first is that Hannibal was born here, and everyone recalls the story of him crossing the Alps on his elephants. The second reason is that Carthage was for a long time the most important city in the Mediterranean, and that means the most important in the western world.

Carthage was probably founded in 814BC by the Phoenicians, from Tyre in modern Lebanon. Their name for it, meaning 'new city' was Qart Hadasht, from which the modern name derives. The Romans attempted to conquer it many times, and only succeeded after first destroying it in 146BC after a three-year siege. It was then re-founded in 44BC and thrived for over 700 years, firstly under the Romans, then the Vandals and finally the Byzantine Empire.

There are six sites spread throughout the area of modern Carthage, but the main one which the organised tours usually take in is that of the Antonine Baths. This is situated on the coast in a pleasant little park, and though there are some other remains on the site, such as a cistern and the remnants of some houses, it is the baths themselves that are the main attraction.

Before you enter the ruins you can see a model of what the baths would have looked like when they were functioning from the 2nd century AD onwards. They were obviously quite spectacular, and were the third biggest baths in the Roman Empire and the largest in North Africa.

You need your imagination to recreate them, and it will help if you have a good guide and/or a good map. You can piece together where the gymnasium was, the changing rooms, the hot, cold and tepid baths, and the central courtyard which was covered by a huge dome supported on twelve pillars, a couple of which still stand with others lying shattered on the ground.

Not far from the baths stood the Roman Theatre, which could once hold 10,000 people and is used today for the annual International Carthage Festival, but the theatre has been almost completely rebuilt and not always in the style of the original.

Further on are the cisterns, which held the water supply brought to Carthage from the spring at Zaghouan thirty-five miles away, but now they are overgrown and neglected. Not far away is the amphitheatre, where 35,000 people once sat to watch the gladiators and wild animals, but their modern excavation has scarcely begun. Carthage still has many secrets it has yet to reveal.

The Antonine Baths at Carthage

HANNIBAL

Born in Carthage in 247BC, by the age of 26 Hannibal was
Commander-in-Chief of the powerful Carthaginian army. No doubt the
fact that his father was a military leader helped a little. He was so
successful that the Romans waged their Punic Wars against the
Phoenicians from Carthage, to try to reduce their power and conquer
them.

It was during the Second Punic War that Hannibal conceived the bold
idea of taking 40,000 troops, with 38 elephants to use as battering rams,
through Spain and France, then across the Alps into Italy, to conquer
Rome by land instead of by the expected sea attack.

Hannibal had several heroic victories but gradually his army
diminished in power and he returned home to defend Carthage, but the
Romans were victorious and a treaty was signed in 201BC. After
further defeats and problems, Hannibal committed suicide at the age of
64.

Hannibal Crossing the Alps

SIDI BOU SAID

This is said to be one of the most beautiful villages in the Mediterranean, and it is certainly up there with the best of them. You might be in the Greek islands or in southern Spain as you explore the narrow streets with their literally dazzling whitewashed houses and blue shutters and doors. In fact you're just about six miles from the bustle and noise of Tunis, perched on a cliff overlooking the Gulf of Tunis.

If you decide you want to live in Sidi Bou Said then you will need to get in a good stock of whitewash and blue paint, as the colours are now legal requirements for house-owners here. They have long got used to the fact that hundreds of tourists visit their village every day, and like to do nothing more than take photographs of their doors and windows.

The large front doors are especially appealing, as they have intricate patterns made from black-painted nails of various sizes. The blue and white palate is broken only by occasional dashes of other colours - the greens of plants or the purple flowers of bougainvillea tumbling over the white walls.

The name of Sidi Bou Said comes from the Arabic word for a Saint, which is Sidi (and is the reason there are so many Sidis in the country), followed by the common Arabic name of Bou Said. Bou Said was a Muslim from the 13th century who was considered to be very holy and who came to settle in the village. He is now buried here and has a mosque named in his honour, to which pilgrims come each August to celebrate the life of Sidi Bou Said.

Sidi Bou Said

SHOPPING

As you would imagine, there are plenty of souvenir stalls and shops greeting you as you step off the coach. However, some of the stuff on offer is rather better than the usual array of carpets and fluffy camels. You might well be tempted by one of the paintings of street scenes or doorways, which can be expensive if you buy an original or much cheaper for a print.

The number of shops and stalls is fairly small when compared to most other tourist attractions, though, so there isn't quite the relentless pestering that you get elsewhere.

The village is also known as one of the places in Tunisia where they make the very ornate bird cages, which you see for sale in many places. The cages, topped with a dome, are made from olive wood and usually painted white, the Muslim colour of peace.

Do find time to explore the back streets, as there are a few shops hidden away from the main throng of visitors, with one or two galleries where you might find an attractive souvenir. You are not limited to views of the village, as the paintings and prints on display also cover other aspects of Tunisian life, and there are sometimes dramatic desert scenes or atmospheric looks at life in the souks and medinas.

THINGS TO SEE AND DO

*** Go along the main street to the headland where there is a lovely view looking down over a small marina and along the coast.

*** Explore the side streets instead of sticking to the main street, as there are some lovely scenes to photograph, with no one else to stand in the way of the view.

BEACHES

People don't usually come to Sidi Bou Said to sunbathe, and on organised excursions there isn't time, but there is a small beach if you continue along the main street.

NABEUL

About eleven miles to the north of Hammamet, and easily reached by bus or taxi, is Nabeul, the main town of the Cap Bon Peninsula. This fertile area of land juts out into the Mediterranean Sea, separating the Gulf of Tunis from the Gulf of Hammamet. It is thought that this is the end of a piece of land which once stretched all the way to Sicily and linked Africa with Europe.

Cap Bon is a green and well-watered area where most of the country's vineyards are situated, as well as extensive groves of orange, lemon and olive trees. Other fruits and vegetables are also grown here, as they have been since before Roman times. The fact that the peninsula is also surrounded by some fine beaches made it an inevitable centre for tourism too.

Nabeul was a busy town long before modern tourism arrived, and so its centre it has a much more Tunisian feel than some of the beach resorts. In fact the town centre is about a mile from the beach area, where the hotels, shops and restaurants have mainly been built, although the two areas are inevitably merging. Nabeul makes a good day out from Hammamet, especially on a Friday when its weekly market attracts visitors from all over the north of Tunisia.

Nabeul

TUNISIA TRAVEL TIP
There's good news and bad news about the Friday market. The good news is that the traders have less time for haggling than usual. The bad news is that this is because the market is so enormously popular that prices are high, there are plenty of visitors who pay them without question, and the traders don't usually need to waste time haggling unless trade is slow.

SHOPPING

Nabeul is where you will find one of the best selections of pottery in the country, as it has been a major centre for ceramics for centuries. The potters here have been influenced by the Phoenicians, the Romans and the Andalucians from southern Spain. As a result there is a bewildering array of choices, from camels on cups to rather more tasteful decorative dishes, especially the local green and yellow ones.

To see examples and prices without having to haggle, pop into the government shop, ONAT, on Avenue Habib Thameur. In contrast, the Friday market is where you may get slightly cheaper prices but only with a struggle.

Nabeul is also known for the production of perfumes, especially jasmine and wild orange flowers: it is in the middle of a fertile orange-growing region. Other local items to look out for include embroidery and woven mats.

THINGS TO SEE AND DO

*** The Friday market. See also under 'Shopping'. This weekly event has developed into one of the major tourist markets in Tunisia, with part of the town closed off to traffic to accommodate the crowds.

* Archaeological Museum. Worth going to if you're keen. The small collection is housed around a courtyard, but the displays are only explained in Arabic and French. You can hire an English-speaking guide for a small tip on top of the entrance fee.

* Neapolis. Also mainly for the enthusiast, this site goes back to the 5th century BC when it was founded by the Phoenicians. Like Carthage, it was destroyed by the Romans and then rebuilt by them. Excavations began in the 1960s but it is rather overgrown in places. A map would be useful but the only one available is attached to a wall in the museum. Ignore the sign which says 'This is closed' but walk down the track to the sea, on the Nabeul side of the sight, as the entrance is there.

BEACHES

The beaches here generally aren't as good as the ones in nearby Hammamet, and the best are the ones that are used by the smart hotels, so if you plan to visit and spend some time on the beaches it is best to pay to use their facilities.

Café in Hammamet

HAMMAMET

Hammamet is the main holiday destination in Tunisia, attracting 30% of all the country's tourists. This makes it a very lively town, with all the amenities you could wish for, including discos, restaurants, good shopping and bars.

It's hardly surprising the town has developed as it has a perfect setting by the sea, with a long sandy beach and a bustling Medina. The houses are attractively whitewashed, and the town is in a fertile region of orange and lemon groves. It's also about halfway between the country's two main airports, and tours both north to Tunis and south towards the desert are equally convenient with Hammamet as your base.

TUNISIA TRAVEL TIP
There are unfortunately many wild cats around some of the hotels, which the authorities are doing their best to deal with by neutering them, with the help of the Society for the Protection of Animals. They may look appealing, but avoid handling them because of the risk of disease, bites or fleas.

SHOPPING
The ancient Medina is the place to go, of course, for the shops and bazaars selling all manner of goods, from nougat and stuffed camels to leather goods and expensive carpets. The further south you go, the more traditional the Medina becomes.

The Commercial Centre in the Centre Ville is one of the shopping areas where you'll find lots of shops together, selling souvenirs, clothes, jewellery, antiques and not-so-antiques.

The local food market is on Avenue de la République, and here you can buy herbs and spices to take home as well as watch the locals stocking up on fresh fish and meat, exotic fruit and veg.

THINGS TO SEE AND DO
*** The Medina. The focal point of any Tunisian town, and the one here dates back originally to the late 9th century, but was rebuilt in the 15th century.

*** The Kasbah. In one corner of the Medina is the Kasbah, or citadel, which has good views from the ramparts. It was first built in the 12th century, rebuilt in the 15th century with the Medina, and has been much restored since then.

** International Cultural Centre. This beautiful 1920s villa to the west of town was the home of millionaire George Sebastian, who invited many of his artistic friends here which started the modern development of Hammamet. The house and grounds are open to the public but check first as international conferences are often held here, when there is no public admittance.

* Pupput. The Roman name for Hammamet was Pupput, and this ruined village can be visited and has some fine mosaics.

BEACHES
There is no shortage of good beaches here, and the two main town beaches are both enjoyable. The one running north-west from the Medina is slightly more attractive and generally more sheltered than the one running north-east.

Dougga

DOUGGA

If you only see one of Tunisia's archaeological sites, make it this one. It is not only the largest and best preserved of the country's Roman remains, it is also the most dramatically set.

This Roman city covers a large part of a hillside, overlooking acres of olive groves in the valley beneath. It is so well preserved that it is quite easy to picture Roman life here, from entertainment in the theatre to entertainment of a different kind in the city's brothel, not to mention worship in the temple and the everyday life in the shops and houses.

You can even still see the ruts made by chariots as they careered through the streets (with anti-skid devices on the street corners), and visit the public latrine, which is actually a lot nicer than many you might see elsewhere in Tunisia.

The most beautiful and imposing building on the site is undoubtedly the Capitol, which is considered to be easily the finest Roman building in North Africa. It dates back to the 2nd century AD, and the temple is dedicated to Jupiter. Viewed head-on, looking towards the three niches at the back of the temple, it is easy to appreciate its geometric perfection.

The first building you come to, however, is the theatre. It is not as big as many other surviving Roman or Greek theatres, but it is excellently preserved and from a seat in the economy rows at the back there is a terrific view of the surrounding countryside. When in use this could hold 3500 people, in 19 rows of seats.

What is best about Dougga, though, is not the grand buildings, which have survived in many other places, but the ones which show the ordinary lives of the people who lived here. The public latrine, for instance, with its near-circle of seats where people could chat as they went about their business. A trough in front of the seats held water which was used for cleaning purposes (you dipped into it with a sponge on a stick), and the sink for washing your hands afterwards also survives.

The houses at Dougga and elsewhere did have their own toilets, and these public ones were partly for the use of visitors or if you were caught short while out in the city, perhaps when on your way to the city brothel, which has also survived. This has a main entrance door, inside which the remains of the cashier's office can be seen, while alongside this is a smaller and more discrete entrance, which was used by the married men. The brothel was on two floors and built around a central courtyard, off which were the necessary small, private rooms.

There are numerous other buildings that survive in very good states of preservation, such as the public baths and various private houses, from which the stunning mosaics have been removed to the safety of the Bardo Museum in Tunis. No matter how long you spend wandering round the site, you can guarantee it will not be long enough.

TUNISIA TRAVEL TIP
Allow extra time for taking lots of photographs as it is a very photogenic site.

VISITING DOUGGA
A tour to Dougga takes a full day and does involve a lot of time spent driving, especially from the southern resorts around Sousse and Monastir. However, it is a journey well worth making and will be broken up by visiting some other remains on the way.

An Old Sketch of Zaghouan
(Looking much as it does today)

ZAGHOUAN

Impressively located beneath the towering slopes of Mount Zaghouan, which at 1295m is the second-highest peak in the country, is the Temple des Eaux, the Temple of the Waters. These ruins are small but their importance was huge in ancient times, as the natural spring here once provided the water for Tunis and Carthage.

The aqueduct to carry the water was almost 45 miles long, much further than the distance as the crow flies, but its circuitous route meant that the water flowed naturally all the way. It was built partly underground and partly on the surface. Remains of this amazing engineering feat can still be seen by the side of the road as you drive along.

THUBURBO MAJUS

All Roman remains in Tunisia pale into insignificance once you have seen Dougga, but the remnants of this Roman city near modern-day El-Fahs are still worth visiting. What you can see today mainly dates back to the 2nd century AD, although there has been a settlement on this site since at least the 5th century BC.

It owes its importance to the produce grown in the area, mainly olives, grapes and grain. The most impressive ruins are those of the Capitol, raised above the city, but other interesting remains are of the two public baths (summer and winter ones), the shops around the market place, mosaics in some well-to-do houses and the Temple of Mercury.

Port El Kantaoui

PORT EL KANTAOUI

With its predominantly white buildings and tastefully-designed white hotels, all surrounding an upmarket Marina, Port el Kantaoui could be almost anywhere in the Mediterranean - Spain, the south of France or the Greek Islands.

It may lack the centuries-old Medina common in other Tunisian towns, but it still has its own North African atmosphere, with cobbled back streets, haggling shopkeepers, waterfront cafés and spicy smells wafting from the many excellent restaurants.

TUNISIA TRAVEL TIP
Just north of Port el Kantaoui on the main road is Sidi Bou Ali, well worth a quick visit to take a look at its folklore centre.

SHOPPING
Port el Kantaoui is one of the best centres for shopping, with many shops selling local craft items clustered around the Marina.

THINGS TO SEE AND DO
There are no tourist sites as such, which doesn't matter too much as Port el Kantaoui is a pleasant place to relax in, and a good base for exploring other parts of Tunisia (see 'Excursions'). What it does have are good sports facilities, including a 27-hole tournament golf course (par 108), and two 18-hole par 72 courses nearby at Palm Links and Monastir.

Sailing: you can either hire your own boat or take a day out on an organised excursion to look at the marine life. A trip along the coast to enjoy the sun and the scenery is easily arranged.

EXCURSIONS
*** Sousse. For a feel of the more traditional side of Tunisia, take the tourist train or a taxi for the five-mile trip to Sousse, with its medina, museum, Great Mosque and many other attractions.

*** Kairouan. Best-reached by taking an organised excursion, Kairouan is one of the country's main centres for traditional carpets, with a chance to see them being made on the weavers' looms.

BEACHES
Long and sandy, as you would expect from a resort built for tourism.

Sousse

SOUSSE

Tunisia's third city has long been a commercial centre and busy port, and with the addition of modern tourism it has become a bustling place to be. It has a huge old town, a good long stretch of beach, and plenty of things to see and do. Because of its size it is still much more Tunisian in feel than many of the smaller resorts, and its long and fascinating history is well worth exploring with visits to the museum, the medina and the fortress.

TUNISIA TRAVEL TIP
If you visit the Ribat it's worth paying the small extra payment for permission to take photos, as there are terrific views from the watchtower.

SHOPPING
Medina. Everyone has to visit the Medina, where the souks sell everything including gold, silver, clothes, spices, meat, fish, fruit and veg.

Soula Centre. A good place for souvenir shopping if you don't like the hassle of haggling, as there's a good range of fixed-price souvenirs on four floors. And it's air-conditioned! Place Farked Hachet in the Centre Ville.

Artisanat Shop. This government-run souvenir bazaar has fixed prices so no haggling. A good place to look at carpets and handicrafts.

Magasin General. Government-run supermarkets, one on La Corniche, the other on Rue de l'Independence, good places for basic toiletries, bits and pieces.

THINGS TO SEE AND DO
***   The Medina. See under 'Shopping'.

*** Sousse Museum. Excellent archaeological museum in the old kasbah in the Medina. Many fine mosaics, with one called the Triumph of Bacchus being a star attraction.

*** The Ribat. Late 8th century fortress in which you must climb the watchtower to get the terrific city views.

** Great Mosque. Looks more like a fortress than a typical mosque, dates back to 851AD but recently restored. Only the courtyard is open to non-Muslims.

* Catacombs. They could be great with over three miles of tunnels, but only a few yards of them are open to the public. Signposted off the Rue el-Ghazali.

BEACHES
Boujaffar Beach is a long strip of white sand where the hotels are, about half a mile north of the city centre. Good watersports facilities, including waterskiing and paragliding.

The Great Mosque at Kairouan

KAIROUAN

To Muslims, Kairouan is known as a holy city, but to visitors it's more like Carpet City. For centuries it has been one of Tunisia's main carpet producers, and is less than an hour's drive inland from Sousse and its neighbouring resorts.

It has a population of about 120,000 and is much more typically Tunisian than the coastal resorts - apart from the daily arrival of coaches bringing visitors to see the sights and perhaps buy a carpet.

The city was founded in 670AD by an Arab General, and its name is said to derive from the Arabic word *qayrawan*, or military camp. However, it is thought that there may well have been a Roman settlement here previously, and the first Arabic settlement was quickly destroyed and it was begun again in 694AD.

TUNISIA TRAVEL TIP
If you're planning any serious carpet shopping, visit Kairouan early in your holiday. Advice from the government-run carpet shop here will make you better-informed and less likely to be taken for a ride in the bazaars. (A carpet ride, presumably.)

SHOPPING
The medina is, naturally, the place to head for your souvenirs but be prepared for a lot of gentle pestering to look into shop after shop, once you've shown the slightest interest in anything. There is also a lot of good-natured banter as you run the gauntlet of shopkeepers.

For less hassle if you're looking for carpets, visit the government-run carpet centre, just to your left after you enter the main gate of the medina. They will advise on quality and prices, have a wide variety of choices from a few pounds to several hundred, and those prices are fixed.

Another good place for buying carpets and other handicrafts is the Centre des Traditions et des Metiers d'Art de Kairouan. This is in the medina on the far side of the covered souks, off the main street. Turn right at the Hotel Bir Baroula along the street of the same name. It is a government-run operation which both sells and demonstrates traditional crafts.

Beware of people who might approach you in the medina and tell you that they are tour guides. They will insist that they will show you the sights and not merely take you to a carpet shop, but then after pointing out the roof of the mosque and the city walls will promptly deliver you to one of the several shops which now call themselves Museums of Carpets.

THINGS TO SEE AND DO

*** The Medina. The old town stands inside city walls that were first erected at the end of the 8th century, although the ones you can see today date mostly from the 18th century. The main street that weaves through the medina from the main entrance gate where the coaches park is mostly lined with souvenir shops, plus some spice stalls and a few cafés. Don't miss the entrance to the covered souks about half-way along on your right. Explore some of the side streets too to find shops where there's slightly less sales pressure.

*** The Great Mosque. There has been a mosque on this site since 670AD, when one was built by the founder of Kairouan, an Arab general named Uqba bin Nafi al-Fihri, and that first mosque was named the Sidi Uqba Mosque. Some locals still refer to it by that name. What we see today dates mainly from the 9th century, and to Muslims it is the fourth holiest mosque in the world, after those at Mecca, Medina and Jerusalem.

** The Mosque of Sidi Sahab.
Not as grand as the Great Mosque but well worth seeing as visitors are allowed along tiled passageways and up stairs to see the mausoleum of Abu Zama el-Belaoui, who was a companion of the Prophet Mohammed and who returned to Kairouan bringing three hairs from the Prophet's beard with him (which are now in Istanbul.) The Arabic word for companion is sahab, hence the mosque's name. It was founded in the 7th century but much of the buildings dates from the 17th century.

* The Aghlabite Cisterns
These two reservoirs were built in the 9th century by the Aghlabites, the dynasty which ruled Tunisia at that time. Water was brought along underground aqueducts from mountains over twenty miles away and stored in thirteen such cisterns, mainly for irrigation purposes. The larger is about 120 yards across and about sixteen feet deep.

Monastir

MONASTIR AND KANES

Monastir was once a small fishing village but has developed with tourism to become one of the most attractive fishing ports in the region. It has a lovely promenade, or Corniche, which runs alongside the beach and blue waters of the Mediterranean, and for part of the way past the high stone walls of the ribat, the town's old fortress.

Monastir was also the birthplace of modern Tunisia's first President, Habib Bourgiba, a national hero whose mausoleum in the town also bears testimony to his importance. He was born in a house on Place 3 August, along the Corniche, and the fact that this was his home town is one reason for its development as a tourist resort and the fact that it's a bustling town with a modern feel to it.

Skanes, just along the coast near the airport, is quieter at the moment but also growing as its hotels attract more visitors. It has a great beach, and good links with both Monastir and nearby Sousse thanks to the Metro service between them.

TUNISIA TRAVEL TIP
It's worth paying the small extra fee for permission to take photos in the Ribat, as there are good views of the town and marina from here.

SHOPPING
You have to try the Medina first, of course, as there are plenty of souvenir shops in among the ones you might not need, like carpenters and cobblers. It's also the place for banks and the supermarket.

The local markets are opposite the Medina off the Avenue Habib Bourguiba, and while you might not want to buy anything it's fun to see the meat, fresh fish, the fruit and vegetables on display.

THINGS TO SEE AND DO
*** Habib Bourgiba Mausoleum
Impressive huge building at northern end of cemetery, beautifully decorated in gold and jade, with two twin minarets. This houses the tombs of the family of modern Tunisia's first President, Habib Bourgiba, but is not open to the public. Well worth seeing, though.

*** Ribat.
This was first built in the 8th century as part of the coastal defences, and was added to and a further defensive wall built in the 9th and 11th centuries. You can see the look-out towers, courtyard, dormitories, a

museum and other features. It has been seen in films as varied as Zeffirelli's Life of Christ and Monty Python's Life of Brian!

*** Medina
Rather different from medinas in other towns, the one in Monastir was partly demolished and modernised. But the people remain, and their stalls and haggling techniques are as fierce and as much fun here as anywhere else. Monastir's big market day is Saturday.

** Grand Mosque
A simple but still impressive example of Islamic architecture, this was built mainly in the 9th and 11th centuries. Dress respectfully if you want to go in and see the courtyard, which is the only part open to the general public.

* Costume Museum
Next to the tourist office in the Medina, this is only small but worth looking into if you're at all interested in the traditional costumes and embroidery of the region.

* Marina
It's worth taking a walk out to the new marina, to dawdle over a coffee in one of the many cafés here (lots of eating places too) while gazing at the luxury yachts and the people who own them.

EXCURSIONS
Monastir and Skanes are ideally placed for exploring the south, including the Roman amphitheatre at El Djem and the cave dwellings at Matmata. It's also only about three hours to Tunis, Carthage and Sidi Bou Said.

BEACHES
The town beach, across from the ribat and the Great Mosque, is excellent if you fancy a change from the hotel swimming pools and beaches, or want to combine swimming with your sightseeing. It's in a sheltered bay thanks to the Marina at one end and the causeway across to El-Kebira island at the other, and has the impressive ribat behind. Quite a setting. The long and sandy beach at Skanes is also good, and ideal for families with young children.

EL DJEM AND MAHDIA

The Roman Amphitheatre at El Djem is one of the most surprising sights in Tunisia. It is almost as big as the Coliseum in Rome, which gives an idea of the town's importance, yet in some ways it is more impressive as it can be seen for miles around and dominates the little houses of this small town. The population today is about 18,000, yet the Coliseum can seat 30,000!

If it were not for the Coliseum, El Djem would be on the itinerary of few tourists to Tunisia. It is a very ordinary small town, in a plane filled with olive trees and whose modern buildings will certainly not be attracting visitors in nearly two thousand years' time.

Mahdia may still be a popular seaside resort, however, and it can be easily combined with El Djem to make quite a contrasting tour. With its medina, mosques and port, Mahdia will remind visitors of the other coastal resorts in this region, but as yet there is not as much tourist development.

THE COLISEUM

This is the largest single Roman ruin in Africa, with three tiers of seating standing almost 100 feet high. It is thought to have been built around 230-238AD by a local landowner named Gordian, who was the African pro-consul to Rome. He even declared himself Emperor of Rome when he was aged eighty, during a rebellion against taxes imposed by the Emperor Maximus. The rebellion was short-lived, as indeed was Gordian as it is said he soon committed suicide inside the Coliseum.

The Coliseum was never actually finished, partly due to lack of funds and partly due to the events that caused Gordian's suicide, but it was much used nevertheless. Its building must have been a monumental task, as the nearest quarries were a good twenty miles away.

Visitors to Gordian's memorial can climb to the top of the rows of seating (making it well worth paying the extra small fee for a camera) as well as exploring the underground passageways where animals were led into the arena to fight against prisoners, or through which the gladiators would walk before facing each other in fights to the death. A good day out for all the family!

TUNISIA TRAVEL TIP

If you want to go to the toilet then use the ones at the Coliseum or in the museum, which are much cleaner than those in the cafés round about.

SHOPPING

El Djem is not a place to shop till you drop. There are the inevitable souvenir sellers, whose prices tend to drop till you shop. In Mahdia you will head for the medina, of course, which is an atmospheric old place, with fewer souvenir stalls than in places such as Sousse and Monastir.

THINGS TO SEE AND DO

*** The Coliseum. See above.

*** The medina in Mahdia. A great place where you step back in time to the old Tunisia.

** The Museum in El Djem. This is about a half-mile south of the Coliseum on the road to Sfax, in a replica of a Roman villa. It is famous for its mosaics, many of them from a villa which once stood next door to the site of the museum. The star exhibit in the main room is 'Orpheus and the Animals', and another one not to miss is one depicting the Nine Muses. Bear in mind that all these came from luxurious Roman villas in the area, which gives you an idea of the opulence of Roman life at that time.

* Salakta Museum, Mahdia. Only small but worth a visit as it has some nice mosaics though not in the same league as El Djem.

BEACHES

It's a long walk to a beach from El Djem, but Medina's beach is to the north-west of town and is as good as any along this coast.

Troglodyte Home in Matmata

MATMATA

This village in southern Tunisia, on the way to the Sahara Desert, is like nothing you have ever seen before. Some of the villagers live underground in homes carved out of the lunar landscape, and have done so for over 700 years. The only sign of modern living is that in some of the homes TV aerials seem to pop up out of the ground!

The Matmata people are Berbers, who have dug out their homes in this way mainly to protect them from the harsh extremes of the climate. In summer the houses are cool when outside temperatures can soar well past the 120-degree mark, and in winter when night-time temperatures fall towards freezing, they can keep themselves snug and warm. The incredibly thick walls keep the temperatures inside at a fairly constant and comfortable 62 degrees. The houses were also good defences against possible invaders.

It's astonishing to witness people still living like this in the 21st century, but the tradition is inevitably slowly dying out as young people move to the coast and the cities, and to overseas, to seek work. If they do return to their home village they often want to build themselves a modern house with all the creature comforts. There is a modern village several miles away called Matmata Nouvelle, or New Matmata. No doubt the houses in the old village will continue as a tourist attraction so that visitors can see this traditional way of life, but at the moment you are still visiting homes where people live.

Several families make their homes available to the public, and are happy for groups to descend on them during the day. It must be a strange feeling to have a few dozen foreigners poking around in your house and peering into the kitchen, but no doubt the dinars they receive help compensate for the intrusion. You may find some of the women putting on weaving demonstrations, or you may just find them cooking lunch, but whichever house you visit and whatever the people happen to be doing, it will be a memorable experience that you will certainly want to photograph.

Each house is usually built around a central courtyard, which you reach through a small door. Most of them have signs painted by the door in blue, like a hand or a fish, to ward off evil spirits. The living quarters are built off the central courtyard, and are kept spotlessly clean, with whitewashed walls and little cupboards and shelves carved out of the rock. Some of the homes are double-deckers, with the upstairs rooms reached by climbing a ladder or just a piece of knotted rope. Some homes have several families and therefore have several inter-connected courtyards, and if you don't happen to visit one of these you can get an idea of what they are like at the three underground hotels in New Matmata, where tour groups often have their lunch.

Some families do have water and electricity supplies, and the TV aerials are obviously evidence of which ones are connected to the electricity supply.

TUNISIA TRAVEL TIP
As usual, have some small change ready. The people who live in these underground houses will expect a few dinars as you pass through, especially if you want to take photographs of them, which they are usually perfectly happy with.

OLIVES
On the way to Matmata you pass the amazing sight of one of the largest olive groves in Tunisia. It contains over two million olive trees, and is roughly twenty miles long and about six to eight miles wide. The crop is harvested in the winter, with each tree producing 75-85 lbs of olives, which in turn make 7-8 litres of olive oil. Tunisia is the third largest grower of olives in the world, after Italy and Spain and ahead of Greece and Portugal. Many of the olives and the oil used to be exported to

Europe, till the advent of the European Union, and now a lot of it goes to the USA.

MAKING MOVIES
Many international movies have been shot on location in Tunisia, and the first Star Wars film used the bleak and unusual landscape around Matmata for some of its locations. The southern deserts were the setting for The English Patient, which resulted in a boost to the country's tourism. In Monastir a studio complex was set up by a relative of President Bourgiba, and this has been used to make a great number of films including Roman Polanski's Pirates, Zeffirelli's Jesus of Nazareth and Monty Python's Life of Brian.

DESERT SAFARIS
The southern part of Tunisia reaches into the greatest desert on earth, the Sahara. It seems a world away from the holiday resorts on the coast, yet it is less than a day's drive to the desert's edges and a town like Douz, often described as 'the gateway to the Sahara'. It would be a foolish visitor who attempted to enter the desert without any experience of driving there, as the few roads that do exist around the edges can easily get covered by sand due to sandstorms. It is therefore all too easy to get lost, and many deaths have occurred among careless visitors.

Nevertheless, it is easy to visit the desert on an organised excursion, and these vary from one-day trips to longer ones of two, three and even more days. Itineraries vary, and a one-day tour only gives a hint of the desert terrain, while longer trips take visitors into areas where roads disappear altogether, and knowledgeable drivers negotiate the sand dunes in four-wheel drive vehicles. Some of the places the tours visit are listed below.

TUNISIA TRAVEL TIP
If you want to buy any dates to take home, then get them in Tozeur. It's renowned throughout Tunisia for producing the best dates you can find anywhere, and it's cheaper to buy them here than elsewhere.

EL DJEM
The town of El Djem with its awesome Roman amphitheatre is on the route to the desert and is often a first stopping-off point. See the entry for El Djem for further information.

MATMATA

The troglodyte village of Matmata is described more fully elsewhere, and it is around here that the first glimpses of the rugged desert terrain can be seen. This is the area of mountain desert, as opposed to the sandy desert further south which is what most people imagine the desert to be. One thing you learn on a desert safari is that sand dunes are only a small part of the experience, although the ones that do exist are even more stunning in reality than any picture can convey.

DOUZ

This small town with its sand-filled streets, its camels and palm trees, is almost at the end of the track. It's a popular spot for tourists, though, as large sand dunes at the edge of the town are an ideal place for a camel ride of an hour or so, giving the visitor the true Lawrence of Arabia feeling. These are often arranged to coincide with either the sunrise or the sunset, and the sunsets in Douz are renowned for their beauty.

Because of the numbers of visitors, the market here does have an increasing number of souvenir stalls such as you might find anywhere, but the big Thursday market is a true Tunisian desert experience, with Berbers from the surrounding village coming into town to buy and sell produce, with a livestock market to go to if you want to buy a camel. Douz is also the place where the International Festival of the Sahara is held each year, with camel-racing, horse-racing and cultural events.

The Chott El-Jerid

CHOTT EL-JERID

The road to Tozeur crosses this vast salt lake, where chemicals in the water affect its colour so that in bright sunlight some stretches can be red, some green and others deep blue. In the afternoon, if conditions are right, mirages often occur too.

MIRAGES

Mirages occur when there are layers of air of various temperatures and densities next to each other. The light rays are bent on the way to the eye so that objects appear in a different place from where they actually are. Some might appear upside down in the sand, so that a patch of sky seems to be water, and in other places you can see objects that might actually be over the horizon. You can photograph mirages but, like the end of the rainbow, you'll never find one.

Sunset in the Date Palms at Tozeur

TOZEUR

There are 200,000 palm trees in Tozeur, making it the second-largest collection of palm trees in the country. This oasis has about 200 natural springs, producing 60 million litres of water every day. A carriage ride takes visitors through the palm trees to take a look at this fertile place, while the little market is also worth seeing, with its fruit, vegetables, fish and meat stalls.

KAIROUAN

Some tours make a stop in Kairouan, before returning to the resort hotels. This is the carpet capital of Tunisia and more information about the town can be found elsewhere in this guide.

THE SAHARA

The vast Sahara Desert, the largest in the world, extends all the way from the Atlantic Ocean and into Iraq, at the far side of the Red Sea. It is about 3200 miles long. From north to south it runs for about 1000 miles, from the shores of the Mediterranean, which it reaches in places, to the Sudan and the River Niger. In total it covers about 3,500,000 square miles, of which only about 2% is in any way fertile, around the various oases.

GENERAL INFORMATION

WHAT'S ON THE MENU

If you love tasty food then you're in for a treat in Tunisia. The country combines the best of Arabic cooking with a healthy influence from the many years of French rule. You can have fish fresh from the sea and grilled to perfection, a wide variety of good fruit and vegetables, mouthwatering if fattening pastries, and all washed down with the surprisingly good Tunisian wine.

The National Dish

This is couscous, which are actually semolina granules. Couscous is a grain which is said to date back to the ancient Berbers and is capable of being served in over 300 different ways. It's steamed over, and usually served with, a stew of lamb, veal or fish, and the Tunisians generally eat it with harissa, a spicy chili sauce. You might want to try just a little harissa first, in case it's too spicy for you as some types are so hot they'll bring the tears to your eyes. If you develop a taste for couscous then look out for a couscoussier to take back home, the traditional dish that it's cooked in.

Couscous, Tunisia's National Dish

Lamb
Lamb is the main meat served in Tunisia, and there may well be 300 ways of cooking this too. You could try coucha, if you see it on a menu: this is shoulder of lamb that's been rubbed in olive oil, salt, pepper, mint and turmeric, and baked slowly in the oven in a sealed earthenware dish. When done it is tender and totally delicious.

Fishy Dishes
Fresh fish is everywhere in Tunisia, and cheap when you compare it to the prices you would pay back home. This, then, is your chance to try red mullet, sea bass, tuna, grouper, perch, sole, simple sardines or squid. Shrimps, prawns and lobster are common too.

Try a Brik
If someone invites you to chew on a brik, then take it. This is another Tunisian speciality, a paper-thin pastry that usually contains an egg with some chopped parsley and meat or fish, frequently tinned tuna. It's then fried and eaten as a snack or an appetiser.

Just Desserts
If you don't fancy the fattening pastries made from nuts and honey - and sometimes they can be a bit too sickly-sweet for some tastes - there is always lots of fresh fruit to finish off a meal, such as oranges, grapes,

melons, dates, pomegranates, medlars, cherries, apricots, plums and many more. Obviously availability is seasonal, and sometimes in early Spring there may not be too much choice, but once the harvests start it'll be rich pickings for the fruit lovers. You can stock up in the markets, although don't forget to give the fruit a good wash before eating it, unless it has a thick peel on it.

ALCOHOLIC DRINKS

Tunisia is a Muslim country and Islamic law forbids the drinking of alcohol. Tunisia has always been a more liberal country than many of its Arab neighbours, though, and because of the large numbers of tourists it takes a pragmatic attitude to alcoholic drinks. They are generally available in restaurants and tourist hotels and can be bought in supermarkets but only between noon and 6.30pm, and not on Fridays, the Islamic holy day. Some restaurants that don't serve wine will allow you to bring your own bottle, so it's worth checking first if you enjoy a glass with your meal.

Celtia is the Tunisian beer that you'll find everywhere, and it's reasonably cheap. More expensive and less common are imported brands or brands brewed under licence in Tunisia, like Stella and Tuborg.

Perhaps surprisingly for an Islamic country, Tunisia has a flourishing wine industry and wine has been made here for more than 2000 years. The white wines tend to be better than the reds, which can be a bit harsh for western palates. The whites are generally dry, and you can also get a selection of rosés too.

Don't forget that the Tunisians are not generally supposed to drink. Some do enjoy a sly tipple, but don't flaunt alcohol in front of them or try to persuade someone to take a drink if they are reluctant.

NON-ALCOHOLIC DRINKS

Tunisia's national drink is tea - but not as we know it! Mostly they drink mint tea, which is very refreshing on a hot day, and if offered some you should never refuse as it is considered discourteous. You may also find green teas and black teas, usually drunk with lots of sugar. If you want British-style tea then ask for a thé au lait (pronounced tay olé) which you should be able to get in most tourist hotels and restaurants. Be warned, though, that it is rarely made with fresh milk.

The Tunisians also love good coffee, and here you should have no problems with expressos, cappuccinos, Turkish coffee and regular coffee all usually available - or at least close approximations of them.

SHOPPING FOR SOUVENIRS
Tunisia is a great place for shopping with a wide choice of souvenirs, from fun items like stuffed camels or simple tee-shirts, through to more expensive hand-made jewellery and traditional carpets.

HAGGLING
Some people are better than others at haggling, but whichever you are you can't deny that it adds to the fun (or stress) of shopping.

If a seller quotes you a price he'll probably be prepared to come down to half that amount, or even less. Try offering a third, which will no doubt cause the seller to protest and tell you how much more the item is worth, but he will also come down a little. Don't immediately meet him halfway: only increase your bid by the amount he came down.

Walking away is one way to tell if the seller really has come down to his lowest price. It might suddenly come down some more, and even if it doesn't you can always wander back later and say you'll take it.

A few things to bear in mind:
* No matter how hard a bargain you think you can drive, the locals do it every day of the week and won't sell you something at a loss.
* If you're tempted to think you paid over the odds for something - well you probably did. But if you like it then just take it home and enjoy it.
* One place not to take shopping lightly is in expensive carpet shops. Once you start negotiating a price, the owner assumes you are seriously interested. He may get annoyed if you stop bargaining and say you've changed your mind, especially if he's spent time showing you things and perhaps offered you tea. Don't start bargaining here unless you do actually want to buy something.

JEWELLERY
Genuine gold and silver items have a hallmark stamped on them: a horse's head, a scorpion or a bunch of grapes. Anklets, bracelets and ear-rings are popular, and the sellers will usually be happy to tell you the significance of the piece you are interested in. Many are traditional Islamic or African designs.

CARPETS
These are best bought in Kairouan, the centre for carpet making where quality is best and prices are cheaper as many carpets originate here. Ask if the carpet has a sealed quality certificate.

LEATHER GOODS
Again, the best place for these is Kairouan. Tunis is also good but has a lot of imported goods from Morocco, which is not necessarily inferior but you don't want your Tunisian souvenir to come from another country, do you? If you're buying leatherware, take a good look at the quality of the stitching, to see if it's sturdy or likely to come apart.

KEEPING CHILDREN AMUSED
Tunisia rightly promotes itself as a good holiday destination for families, and there will be no problem at all in keeping the children amused and occupied. From a practical point of view, the local supermarkets are usually well-stocked with items you might need, like nappies and baby-food.

No Shortage of Watersports for Children in Tunisia

ON THE BEACH

Most of the country's main beaches are equipped with good watersports facilities, so while younger children can enjoy simply splashing about and playing in the sand, older ones who are confident swimmers might want the challenge of learning to water-ski or going paragliding. In some resorts you can hire boats by the day too.

EXCURSIONS

Children love any form of transport and one thing to bear in mind if you want to take a bus or train somewhere yourself is that children under five travel for free, and children under fifteen travel for half price. The classical side of Tunisia - sites like Carthage and El Djem - are probably best left for children old enough to appreciate them but, even so, younger children can get a surprising amount of fun from running around old ruins.

NODDY TRAINS

These trains link the hotels in some resorts with the town centre, and are a leisurely way of getting around. Sometimes they are very leisurely, and don't always stick to the timetable, so don't take them if you want to be somewhere by a particular time. Children love rides on these, so much so that you'll probably have to ration them.

CAMELS

Taking a ride on a camel is something that everyone responds to - if only with a blank refusal to do it! Getting the kids on a camel is always a source of great amusement, and it's even more fun when the kids insist that mum and dad try one too. This is definitely an event when you should make sure you have your camera ready with a fully-charged battery. The Camel Caravan is one event that's a must for young children.

EATING OUT

Like most people around the Mediterranean, the Tunisians love children and love making a fuss of them. It's more common here to see everyone dining together as a family, and children will enjoy being treated as grown-ups. Waiters often make a special effort with children, enjoying a joke when they're not too busy.

ACTIVITIES IN TUNISIA
WATERSPORTS
Almost all the hotels have their own section of beach, and many provide various watersports activities too. The prices are cheap compared to back home and some other places in the Mediterranean, so here's your chance to try it. Among the options you should be able to find are waterskiing, paragliding, windsurfing and simpler fun things like banana boats and pedaloes.

Tunisia Has Many Golf Courses

GOLF
For those people who thought Tunisia was all desert - well it isn't just one big bunker! There are several fine golf courses, though the keen

golfers will have followed advice and pre-booked their tee-off times before leaving home. It might still be possible to find a space, though, even if you've left it to the last minute. You technically need your handicap certificate with you, but if the greens are not too busy they may be prepared to bend the rules.

CYCLING
Hiring a bike is an increasingly popular way of getting about, despite the fact that Tunisians are, shall we say, enthusiastic drivers. You might want to get used to cycling on quiet side streets before tackling the busy main roads. The standard of bikes used to be pretty basic, but they are getting better as the demand increases.

HORSE RIDING
Some hotels offer horse riding facilities, while if you want to watch horse racing there is a course at Monastir.

FISHING
Anyone interested in deep-sea fishing, perhaps for shark, tuna or swordfish, can usually find someone willing to take you by asking around the Marina, if there are no formal trips on offer. You need a permit for river fishing in Tunisia, but not for sea fishing.

FOOTBALL
Soccer is the country's number one sport, and the national side has qualified twice for the World Cup finals. There are several first division sides in Tunis, and another in Sousse, if you want to try to catch a good game.

A SPOT OF CULTURE
Tunisia has more than enough by way of cultural interest to satisfy anyone, and even if your aim is to spend most of your holiday lying in the sun you will still find yourself surrounded by Arabic culture the moment you walk into any of the bazaars. Buying, selling and more particularly haggling, is a way of life here, and seeing the buzz and bustle is a long way removed from a visit to your local supermarket.

ISLAMIC CULTURE
Never forget that you are in a Muslim country, where people have always dressed modestly and where the sight of someone in a swimsuit is a very recent thing. Keep the bikinis for the beach, although people in tourist towns are now well-used to seeing visitors wandering round in their shorts and t-shirts. However, if you know you might be visiting

a mosque on one of your days out, dress appropriately: no shorts, no bare shoulders. And if taking a day trip to more out-of-the-way places, again dress more respectably. In these places, men wearing shorts are thought to be walking round in their underwear!

ROMAN REMAINS

If your interest is in ancient history, you could spend all your holiday looking round the country's archaeological sites, and still only skim the surface of them. Many are not easily accessible from the coastal resorts, but you should certainly not pass up a chance to visit those that are nearby. The name of Carthage is known to everyone, and is probably a 'must' on most people's itineraries, being now a virtual suburb of Tunis. Slightly less well-known is El Djem, yet the remains of this Roman Coliseum are almost as good as the Coliseum in Rome. The Roman ruins of Dougga are probably the best-preserved in the country, in an impressive isolated setting, and are a 'must' for anyone remotely interested in history.

DESERT CULTURE

To get a feel for the true history of Tunisia, you must make a trip into the desert. To see the way that the Berbers and other desert dwellers live is a revelation after indulging in the pleasures available to visitors on the coast. In fact simply seeing the desert is an eye-opener for most people. It is far from being the endless sweeps of sandy dunes that we expect, but is much more varied, and no-one who takes a trip into the desert ever forgets the experience.

TUNISIAN TRAVELS
Three Travel Pieces by Mike Gerrard

TUNISIA BY TAXI

It was the strawberries that did it. Our jovial driver Mokaddem pulled
up by the roadside on the way back to Tunis, and returned to his taxi
clutching a bulging carrier bag. With a smile he showed us his swag,
enough strawberries to feed the Centre Court crowd at Wimbledon for
a fortnight. He handed us some and, with typical courtesy, also passed
us some tissues to mop up the juice.

We were on the Cap Bon peninsula, just south of Tunis, in a landscape
that is like a mix of the vineyards of Italy and the olive groves of
Greece. The occasional red-roofed and dazzling white farmhouses are a
reminder too of its Andalucian connections, with settlers from Spain
having joined earlier groups like the Romans and Carthaginians. They
came to conquer and were themselves conquered by what they found
here. Cap Bon paints the more Mediterranean picture of Tunisia, which
many people associate only with beaches and desert.

We had wanted to see Cap Bon while we were in Tunis, but one look at
Tunisian driving, and a second look at car hire rates, made us reluctant
to do it ourselves. We were north of Tunis in the beach resort of
Gammarth, and Cap Bon was south. Between us lay the city, which has
many attractions but the traffic isn't one of them. A typical street is the
4-wheel equivalent of shoppers storming a department store on the first
day of the sales.

Enter at 9am our knight in shining armour, Mokkadem, recommended
by one of the hotel staff and who would put himself and his Mercedes
at our disposal for a very modest amount. We'd been assured he spoke
English, though 'no problem' was the main phrase he used. Fiftyish and
obviously no fan of the Hip and Thigh Diet, he steered us south. His
glove compartment had no door on it, and was stuffed with cassette
tapes. Stacked neatly in piles, they filled every available inch, and we
were soon relaxing to the gentle strains of Arabic music.

At Soliman he stopped to refill his coffee cup, and bought us a bottle of
cold water, welcome in the 80-plus heat. He waved away my offer to
pay. A few miles later we were in Korbous, a spa town since Roman
times where, on the edge of town at the enticingly-named Goat Spring,
water gushes from the mountainside and pours over rocks into the sea.

In the turquoise waters, a group of boys were splashing and laughing, waving at our cameras.

'Come, touch the water,' said Mokkadem, leading us to the spring itself. We put our fingers in the flow and jumped back, the water scalding hot as it pumped from the earth. We head back for the car, our driver temporarily diverted by a stall selling cassettes. He can't resist the temptation to buy one, and puts it with glee in his tape player.

On to El Haouaria, next town down the coast, where a network of 100 caves were first quarried for their sandstone almost 3,000 years ago. Inside the entrance we're greeted by an enthusiastic young guide. Tunisia is full of these, some official and some unofficial, some good, some atrocious. I remember visiting Tunis's Bardo Museum on a previous occasion and politely turning away a guide by the entrance. He was affronted that I should not want his services. 'I am qualified guide,' he told me, brandishing a permit, 'I am not some rubbish from the street!' Impressed by his English, I hired him, and didn't regret it.

We hired this young guy too, who led us through the caves with a torrent of enthusiastic information. 'These caves quarried by 30,000 black slaves from south of Africa, black, black, and tied together, 30,000, look, see...' He crosses his hands to indicate manacles, shows us niches in the walls where they were imprisoned, the holes in the rooves where the huge slabs of rock were winched out and taken by boat to Carthage, the cave where the dead slaves were buried. The whole story comes alive as he relates with enthusiasm a tale he must have told a thousand times before.

We return to Mokaddem's Mercedes exhilarated but exhausted. Again we hit the road, to spend an hour at Kerkouane, Tunisia's most impressive Punic ruins, and on to Kelibia, where a massive 6th-century Byzantine fortress guards the harbour. We're rather disconcerted to find a cow inside, and several chickens, but then discover that the caretaker lives on the premises, so that's all right. Mokkadem has gone into town to eat a late lunch, and is waiting for us by the gate as promised an hour later. As we flop onto the back seat, wilting in the heat, we're grateful that we now don't have to spend the next two hours driving ourselves back to Tunis. When we eventually approach it close to 7pm, Mokkadem explains it's the rush hour, so he skirts round the centre, takes us on a ferry, and delivers us back to our hotel safe and sound. We've already booked him for the next day too, having decided that touring Tunisia with a driver like Mokkadem is definitely better than driving yourself or taking an organised coache trip. And you get free strawberries too.

ON THE TUNISIAN FRONTIER
The road sign by the roundabout in the middle of town points to the Algerian Frontier. This is Tunisia, where French is the second language, and the very word Frontière sounds exotic, with its suggestion of exploration and adventure, of new worlds. Border, on the other hand, sounds too like Barrier.

We are in the mountain town of Ain Draham, in western Tunisia. It isn't totally unchartered territory, but it isn't charter flight territory either. To get here we left behind the sophisticated chaos of Tunis, and first drove northwest to one of the most surprising sights in the country: Lake Ichkeul. It's surprising because in this country that borders the Sahara, Ichkeul is a lake covering 23 square miles and is one of only two UNESCO protected biosphere reserves in the world. The other is the Florida Everglades.

Ichkeul is also the most important bird sanctuary in North Africa, providing a winter home for almost a quarter of a million waterbirds. However, on a hot afternoon in September we have to limit ourselves to a visit to the small museum and be content with the sight of a few stuffed ducks and eagles. More impressive are the dozens of water buffalo we see grazing in the reed beds, and other mammals here include porcupine, giant otter, foxes, jackals, and wild boar.

Wild boar are also common in the cork oak forests that surround Ain Draham, 60 miles west of Lake Ichkeul, where we hire a local guide named Yahia to take us for a walk in the woods. He wears a jaunty safari hat at a rakish angle, and is a wiry 52-year-old who lopes along in trainers, managing to move at great speed without appearing to expend any energy. He brings along his fox terrier, Osiris. We're scarcely a minute into the walk, still in the dusty back streets of the town, when Yahia plucks a dandelion from the roadside and sings its praises to us. It's a great source of Vitamin C, he says, and a valuable medicinal plant: 'C'est une plante très intéressante.'

As we leave the houses behind it becomes clear that Yahia finds everything 'très intéressante', and so too does Osiris. Osiris chases cats while Yahia points out juniper trees and cherry trees, and tells us we can ask him questions on any subject but politics. On plant life he needs no asking. The flowers of the blackberry bush are very good for gum problems, he informs us, while a tablespoon of bramble jelly will help you see better at dawn and dusk. We walk on into the dense and shady cork oak woods, where Yahia points out the trunks partly stripped of their bark. Cork is one of the economic mainstays of this valley, 3000ft up in the Kroumirie Mountains on the Algerian border, where Tunisia's last lions and leopards were shot a hundred years ago. Hunting is still a big attraction, as Yahia explains.

'In winter we get the German visitors. They just want to shoot all day and drink all night.' They pay good money, and there is no shortage of wild boar in the area. In fact, says Yahia, there will be one sleeping about 200 yards from where we have stopped.

'They are mainly nocturnal. They don't attack people except during the mating season or when one of them is hurt. Then you have to take care. But you should take a cigarette with you into the woods, as the boar don't like the smoke.'

We stop in what could be an autumnal glade in an English woodland, where Yahia points out tiny golden mushrooms, scarcely bigger than a pin-head. There is a wild lavender plant too, and myrtle trees. We emerge from the wood in what could be the North Yorkshire Moors, a hillside covered in browning ferns. Fern Mountain, says Yahia, and at the top we get our first glimpse of Algeria, a few miles away. On the gentle slopes of a hill mirroring ours stands a village of square white houses. Yahia's sister lives there, married to an Algerian man, and he goes to visit them almost every week.

As we walk down again and back into the bracken, we ask if there are any snakes around. 'Just a few friendly ones,' Yahia assures us. 'The boars eat the rest.'

We continue driving south, hugging the Algerian border, till we see a sight that few visitors to Tunisia ever see, and which few people know anything about. Jugurtha's Table is an astonishing flat-topped mountain whose sheer sides rise out of the surrounding plain to a height of 4170ft. It looks like a huge fountain of rock shooting straight to the heavens. A 2-hour walk from the nearest village, Kalaat Es Senam, takes you round the side of the mountain to the rear where, carved out of the rock face, is a series of stone steps, the only way up to the top of this vast landscape.

We haul our aching legs up, our expensive walking boots clumping on the stone, our lungs pounding. We stop for a break to catch our breath, and at that moment a Tunisian man approaches us on the downward path. He is at least 70, leaning on a stick to support his bad leg, and wearing a pair of carpet slippers. 'You are walking too fast,' he tells us. 'Take it slowly. Of course these days I have to do it slowly because of my leg. I can't get about like I used to.'

And with that he waves us cheerily on and we ascend, more slowly, to the top of this bizarre feature. The scenery here looks like the rugged American west with its mesas, and a bit like the moon. They film Star Wars in Tunisia, and if Jugurtha's Table hasn't featured yet it's only because George Lucas hasn't discovered it. It's a secret other planet on the rocky top, which extends for miles in every direction. Sheep graze in the distance, like animals on the African plain. Thousands of white-shelled snails are clinging to the scraggy plants and bushes. A few well-fed wheatears flit among the rocks.

Without speaking, the three of us who have climbed up here all go our separate ways, overawed by the place, seeking some solitude to try to make sense of it all. Not that we could, as no-one knows the full story of this imposing plateau. Jugurtha was a Numidian king who dug in on the top of this mountain to resist the Romans for seven years in the 2nd century BC. It has since been the home of bandits and Byzantines. Crumbled ruins on top could be churches or mosques.

I climb over a wall into a courtyard, where pillars have fallen. I never fail to see a fallen pillar without imagining the crash as it thundered to the ground. In the centre of the courtyard stands a small pile of stones, with a flat-topped stone like a hat on the top. Arranged on this are a few coloured pebbles, looking very paganistic, like New Age worship in this age-old place.

I walk towards the edge of the plateau, jumping across fissures in the rock, as if the earth had tried to rip the Table apart but failed. I keep a respectful distance from the edge. The sky darkens in the distance, and thunder rumbles. The whole feeling is Biblical, apocalyptic. I expect a plague of frogs to start raining down. In front of me may be the frontier with another country, Algeria, but up above my head I feel a frontier with another world.

Entrance to the Bardo Museum

AT THE BARDO MUSEUM

'I am not rubbish off the street,' Said told me indignantly when I initially turned down his offer to guide me round Tunis's Bardo Museum. After all, I'd been briefly before, had my Rough Guide with me with its excellent museum map, and had the whole day if I wanted it. 'I am a qualified guide,' said this smart-suited man, with his glasses, bushy moustache and dapper red fez. He showed me his Tourist Guide papers. 'You cannot get a guide inside the Museum, and I can tell you things you will not read in the books. Only ten dinars for one hour, two hours, as long as you wish!' A few pounds? It was a deal.

I'd been bowled over by the Bardo on a brief guided tour as part of 'A Day in Tunis' when staying in one of Tunisia's beach resorts the previous year. It has the world's finest collection of Roman mosaics, but is one of those rare museums which would be worth seeing even if stripped of all its contents. The building is the former Bardo Palace, home to the Beys or Regents of Tunis, and there has been a Palace on the site since the 13th century. The present white Moorish building dates back to the end of the 17th century, and has been a museum since 1888.

'Look at the beautiful blue tiles, look at the stucco ceiling,' Said instructed me as we wandered round. I'd decided to put myself into his hands for now, enjoying his occasionally fractured English ('This is Emperor Hadrian, the founditor of Carthage Baths') and the way his character illuminated his descriptions: 'Here we see a mosaic of a lion attacking a horse. It is the sight of tyranny, no? The strong always wishes to devour the weak.'

The Bardo's collection of mosaics is astonishing in both its scope (much of the museum's three floors is given over to them) and its quality. One reason for this is that Tunisia's hot, dry climate preserved them particularly well, and another is that the North African trend was for multi-coloured floor mosaics to contrast plain-coloured walls, while the fashion on the Mediterranean's northern shores was for colourful walls and monochromatic floors.

Some floors, too. The largest mosaic is 140 square metres, from the floor of the reception hall of a wealthy horsebreeder from Sousse, which shows Neptune surrounded by sea creatures. The most detailed items are four small mosaics called emblemata. These are made up of fragments as small as 2mm, giving an almost photographic quality to them. The best shows the remains of a meal, including fishbones and egg-shells. 'All natural colours,' Said explained, 'no painting, no dyes, just stone, minerals, glass, terracotta, all these kinds of things. Truly the work of skilled artists.' Indeed, and a reminder that mosaics, like music, owe their name to the muses.

I paid off Said with a cup of coffee and a tip. 'Many people are so pleased with my tour that they give me a tip, but of course I never ask for one,' he had clarified for me, in case I was unsure. I was free to wander round more leisurely, and argue with the Rough Guide. The author dismisses the El Djem Room in one sentence, as containing 'hunting scenes to delight the heart of any blood-sport enthusiast' - a strange way to understand the past, by filtering it through the sensibilities of the present. It's not even true. The El Djem Room has a couple of hunting scenes and several dozen exquisite wildlife mosaics showing fish and fowl, gazelles, hares, fruit and flowers.

One thing everyone agrees on is that a star exhibit is the 3rd century mosaic of the poet Virgil, which on my previous tour the guide had unashamedly described as 'the finest mosaic in the world.' Today a British tour group is gazing at it like a Tunisian Mona Lisa, and the guide says: 'Your Queen of England came to see this mosaic and she stood gazing in wonder at it for thirty minutes, such is its beauty.' Yes, well, even if you can only spare five minutes, you can still appreciate its almost perfect state of preservation, and incredible detail: you can even read a line from the Aeneid on the papyrus scroll that Virgil is holding in his lap.

In the end, in all museums, despite the experts and the guides and the books telling you what are the best things in the collection, you will always find the little things that move you more than anything. I was looking not at the magnificent mosaics but at the humbler terracotta pieces in display cabinets around the balconies that look down on the Carthage Room. At the far end, in the central cabinet, was a relaxing - or should that be resting? - actor with a face so wonderfully awful that it cheered me up no end. Then I took a look in the final cabinet and there was a head, a few inches high, of a beautiful chubby-cheeked baby, its gurgling grin almost lost between the fat folds of its face. What skill, I thought, to make that child come alive two thousand years later. Then I glanced at the caption, one of the few in English, and saw that it was a funeral mask. I made my way downstairs to the exit.

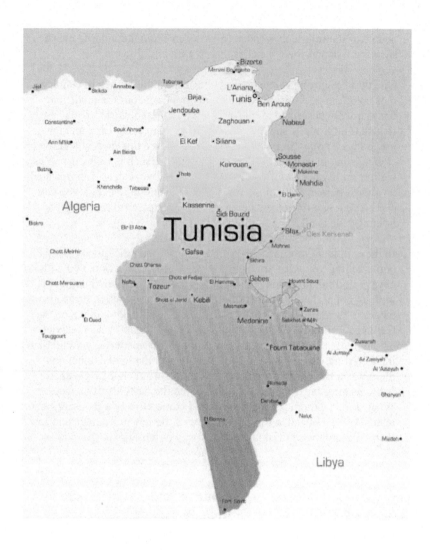

El Djem

The Sahara Desert in Tunisia

Riding Horses on the Beach at Djerba

Camel-Racing at the International Festival of the Sahara in Douz

Bread for Sale at a Tunisian Market

Camel on a Tunisian Beach

Tunisia Has Lovely Ceramics

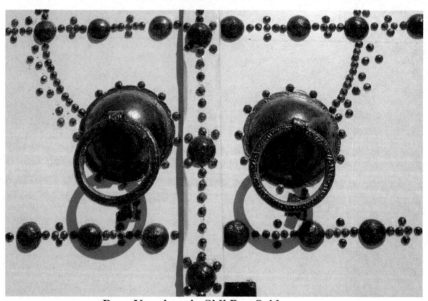

Door Knockers in Sidi Bou Said

Tunisian Window

Tunisian Woman with her Jewellery

INDEX

I

J

K

L

M

N

O

P

R

S

T

V

W

Z

If you enjoyed this book then please consider leaving a review on Amazon. It helps publishers, authors, and buyers alike.

Printed in Great Britain
by Amazon

28331682R00044